GUN CAMERA
PACIFIC

L. DOUGLAS KEENEY

MBI Publishing Company

First published in 2004 by MBI Publishing Company, Galtier Plaza, Suite 200, 380 Jackson Street, St. Paul, MN 55101-3885 USA

MBI Publishing Company books are also available at discounts in bulk quantity for industrial or sales-promotional use. For details write to Special Sales Manager at Motorbooks International Wholesalers & Distributors, Galtier Plaza, Suite 200, 380 Jackson Street, St. Paul, MN 55101-3885 USA. Library of Congress Cataloging-in-Publication Data Available

ISBN 0-7603-1758-5

On the front cover: High among the cumulus clouds, B-29s bomb the city of Kobe, Japan. The city was targeted for its numerous factories supporting the Japanese war effort.

On the frontispiece: On February 1, 1945, 12 B-25s knock out Mong Pawn bridge as 28 fighter-bombers support ground forces around Hosi and Molo in Burma.

On the title page: Screaming through a fusillade of antiaircraft fire, a Japanese Jill bomber bears down on the fleet near Truk. However close she appears, the plane was destroyed before releasing her torpedo. This exceptionally clear, two-shot series captures the intensity of war at sea and the ferocious hail of fire that came up to meet Japanese and Navy flyers alike.

On the contents page: A Japanese Sally bursts into flames after being hit by bullets from the guns on a Navy Liberator.

On the back cover: Her engine streaming fire and smoke, a Mavis goes down.

Edited by Steve Gansen
Designed by Rochelle Schultz

All photographs courtesy of the National Archives and Records Administration, Archives II, College Park, MD.

Printed in China

CONTENTS

CHAPTER 1

AIR WAR PACIFIC

The war in the Pacific began with a carrier-launched air attack against Pearl Harbor and ended after two atomic bombs obliterated the Japanese cities of Hiroshima and Nagasaki. In between? Almost four solid years of fighting so savage that battles would end only when an opposing force had been completely annihilated or, barring that, evacuated in the dark of night.

Guadalcanal. Bougainville. New Guinea. The Philippines. Tarawa. Eniwetok. Guam. Iwo Jima. From the initial landings until the islands had been declared secure, campaigns could often be measured in days or scores of days. That was not the way of war in Europe. But that was the way it was in the South Pacific. Intense. Concentrated. Battles that were fought to the bitter end.

After a string of penetrating advances made by the Japanese in 1941 and 1942, the road to Tokyo was a daunting 2,600 miles long. Pushed back to Australia, Army General Douglas MacArthur would be forced to lead a difficult ground advance up through the Japanese-held jungles of New Guinea to the Philippines. Navy Admiral Chester W. Nimitz, with his extraordinarily talented task force commanders, fought up through the South and Central Pacific—island hopping with his carriers and marines from Guadalcanal to Bougainville, then back northeast through the Marshalls, Gilberts, and Marianas. From there, MacArthur and Nimitz would join forces and together take the Philippines, then Iwo Jima and Okinawa where, looking across the

Right: Marines watch the progress ashore during the invasion of Iwo Jima. Mt. Suribachi is in the background. Iwo Jima would be one of the bloodiest battles in the Pacific but the air bases there would prove to be of incalculable value. Not only would land-based fighters on Iwo Jima provide cover to the B-29s attacking Japan, but Iwo Jima also proved to be a life saver as an alternate airstrip for bombers that needed to divert or land early. In just six months, between March 1945 and the end of the war, over 2,400 B-29s put in at Iwo, saving untold numbers of lives.

space of 400-miles of ocean, they faced the Japanese mainland itself.

Under General Henry A. "Hap" Arnold, and with the brilliant leadership of his commanding generals, particularly General George C. Kenney, commander of the Fifth Air Force, bombers and fighters moved forward into the Pacific as new bases were secured. The overall objective was to take Guam, Tinian, and Saipan, from which B-29s would then mount the air offensive against mainland Japan. To protect the B-29s, fighters would be edged forward to positions on Iwo Jima, while Okinawa would be secured to provide a marshalling point for the invasion of Japan itself. To protect the rear, garrison air forces were stationed on the newly liberated islands. This then became the character of the air war: Advance. Protect the gains. Advance again. Strike Japan.

In a macroscopic view, this was the war in the Pacific but as any soldier knows, wars are not macroscopic. Wars are intensely personal—one airplane, one bullet, one twist of fate or trick of timing separating life and death. It was in these precious units of one that men lived or died and no quarter was given as each side fought with unwavering tenacity. Through the smothering heat and the snake-infested jungles, men clawed their way forward and fought a fanatical enemy with every weapon they had—flamethrowers, hand grenades, machine guns, pistols, artillery, the cold steel of knives and bayonets, and their bare hands. They engaged the enemy in tunnels, in the jungles, at sea, and in the sky. They were picked off with deadly accuracy by snipers perched in the tree tops, then pushed to their physical and emotional limits by waves of

Japanese charging the lines with the bone-chilling cry of *"Banzai!"* most to be cut down by murderous fields of inter-lacing machine gun fire. At sea, the ships maneuvered with tactical brilliance (and in some cases, gross miscalculations) but the punctuation mark would be the horrifying sight of a suicide bomber, later known as the kamikaze, boring in towards a ship. In Okinawa alone, the Japanese mounted more than 800 air raids with more than 4,000 aircraft, no less than 2,000 of

which were kamikazes, all of them to be lost, some stopped by antiaircraft fire, some to fighters, others by plunging into the decks of their targets, sinking or damaging 191 ships.

What made this war so personal? More than meets the eye. While the near deification of a soldier that sacrificed his life for his country was indeed a powerful force in the psyche of the Japanese solider, the war in the Pacific was also fueled by racial currents, currents that existed on both sides but in quite different ways. On our part, revenge against the enemy that killed our men at Pearl Harbor was a motivator that intensified as we bore witness to the enemy's almost inhuman conduct in combat. The Japanese soldier literally fought to the death—if not in combat, then by choosing suicide over surrender. Of the 4,700 Japanese on Tarawa, only 17 were taken prisoner; on Kwajalein, all but 30 died out of a garrison force of 8,000. From a military standpoint, the deaths were senseless, but for the American soldier probing the bodies around a bunker, a hidden hand grenade clutched in the hands of a wounded Japanese soldier confirmed all fears and triggered angers most men never before felt. Many an otherwise simple, God-fearing American boy fought with the passionate, guttural cry to remember Pearl and, in the most contemptuous of exhortations, to "Kill a Jap! Kill more Japs!" It was a battle cry repeated until the end of the war.

For the Japanese, racism ran even deeper. Americans were little more than human detritus. When our forces surrendered, which we did in the Philippines, or were captured, our men were treated with gruesome inhumanity; causalities among prisoners were horrendous—seven times the death rate in the European theater. If a man was weak and unable to walk or feed himself, he was shot. If a man was slow to obey an order, he was beaten. If it suited their captors, prisoners were beheaded, or, in one particularly loathsome atrocity, burned in a pit soaked in gasoline. It was a pattern of cruelty that began with the capture of the first American prisoners of war,

B-29s encounter flak over Nagoya, Japan.

the survivors of Lieutenant Colonel James H. Doolittle's April, 1942 raid on Tokyo, three of whom were executed.

The intensity of the fighting defined this war and it was felt in the air, too, for control of the skies meant certain victory and both sides knew it. The jungles were harsh and the islands had no natural resources. Isolated by thousands of square miles of ocean, resupply was essential to survival, much less winning the battles. With control of the skies, Allied forces could interdict the Japanese convoys of foods, medicines, and munitions so desperately needed by the diseased and heat-ravaged jungle fighters. On the other hand, without control of the skies, the air bases so perilously held by the Allies would be little more than meat grinders—Zekes and Bettys and Vals, if not opposed, could sweep in to pummel the fields and rip to shreds the miserable tent barracks with flesh-clawing fragmentation bombs.

To prevent that, we attacked enemy airfields to destroy their aircraft and engaged the enemy in air-to-air combat. Full-fledged aerial battles were so intense that aces would be made in a day, and several times at that. Three-hundred enemy aircraft were shot down in one day in the Marianas. The top air ace of World War II, Army Major Richard I. Bong, flew in the Pacific and had 40 victories. Major Thomas McGuire, also a USAAF pilot in the Pacific, had 38. The Navy's top ace was Commander David McCampbell, with 34 kills in the Pacific, and the Marine's top ace, Captain Joe Foss, had 26, also in the Pacific. (Captain Francis "Gabby" Gabreski, the leading air ace in Europe, had 28 kills.)

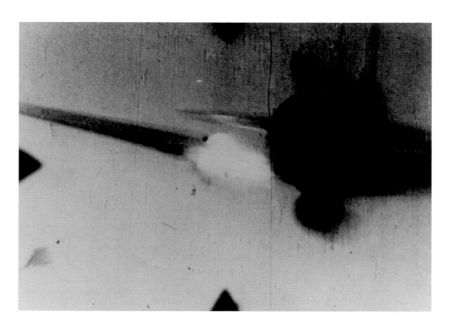

An impressive, nearly head-on gunnery pass—a Japanese Zero in the sights of a P-38.

Navy dive bombers leave behind the burning hulks of Japanese ships interdicted along the coast of French Indochina.

The need to control the skies dictated much of the progress of the war. Islands were targeted, attacked, and invaded precisely because they had airfields, or because airfields could be built on them. We secured Henderson Field on Guadalcanal; Tarawa, Eniwetok, Kwajalein, New Georgia, and Bougainville were taken. We took Saipan, Guam, and Tinian for our bombers, and Iwo Jima for our escort fighters. More than 100 air bases were built or occupied on Pacific islands, not including those in Australia, India, Burma, China, and Indonesia. Some were little more than muddy or dusty coral airstrips; others were airfields with numerous parallel runways with bombers in revetments as far as the eye could see.

Carrier aviation was integral, too, and the number of carriers in the Pacific grew rapidly from just six fleet carriers at the onset of the war to more than 130 fleet, light, and escort carriers by war's end. How valuable were they? Tarawa was attacked by 14 aircraft carriers with 900 planes. Eighteen escort carriers and several larger carriers with more than 1,000 planes supported the landings on Leyte. During the campaign for Okinawa, 31 carriers provided tactical air support—and from the decks of aircraft carriers would be launched the first American thrusts into the Pacific. The Battle of the Coral Sea took place on May 6 to 8, 1942 near Australia, and, while it was militarily indecisive, it halted the Japanese advance into Port Moresby, New Guinea and thus kept open our supply routes to Australia. Next came Midway, a battle so profound and, with four Japanese aircraft carriers sunk, so clearly an American victory that historians would in hindsight say that it signaled the end of the war. Not that any end was yet in sight. What followed was the invasion of Guadalcanal, which would not be decided for six months, not until all of the Japanese forces were either killed, captured, or evacuated. After Guadalcanal the land, air, and

Living conditions in the Pacific differed markedly from those in Europe. Below, marine pilots of the 2nd Marine Aircraft Wing mill about their tents near the airfield on Peleliu while on the facing page, bottom right, marines on Guadalcanal suffer the furnace-like heat of a scorching day. Either way, it was a far cry from the housing in England or the villages of France.

sea forces would function like a claw—one side encompassing New Guinea to the south and the other the Central Pacific islands to the north—until the pincers closed at Luzon more than two years later.

Air power was the decisive factor in the Pacific, a truth acknowledged even by the admirals of the United States Navy, whose pride in their ships knew no bounds. The first assault against the Philippines in 1944 included 730 planes. Fighters shot down 1,067 of the 4,000-plus aircraft the Japanese brought to save Okinawa (artillery and antiaircraft fire downed another 900). General Kenney's Fifth Air Force

P-51s arrive in Guam. It was standard practice to load the guns before the planes were hoisted ashore. From Guam, these P-51s were flown to Saipan and then on to Iwo Jima where they would be based and fly escort missions with B-29s. The USAAF provided garrison forces in the rear areas and escort fighters in the forward areas. In rear area actions Army fighters not only protected islands retaken by the Allies, but attacked the bypassed Japanese-held islands such as Rabaul.

Seen here lining runways in the Marianas, B-29s were nothing less than an audacious display of America's industrial and military might. By the end of the war in the Pacific, more than 2,000 B-29s were in active service.

claimed over 150 aircraft destroyed on the ground during one day of fighting at Wewak, and eight weeks later ravaged the Japanese again at Rabaul, claming another 150 planes or more. During the entire war, Navy and Marine Corps aviators destroyed 15,401 Japanese aircraft on the ground. On its side, the Army Air Corps destroyed 10,343 aircraft on the ground. In air-to-air engagements, America lost 2,421 aircraft—but downed 16,611 of the enemy's.

Air power was no less decisive against convoys and surface combatants. Six of Japan's 12 battleships and 12 of Japan's 20 aircraft carriers were fatally struck and primarily sunk by aircraft (with some assists to submarines and surface ships). Unassisted aircraft sank over 2,000,000 tons of Japanese vessels, not including the hundreds of small barges, sampans, and luggers used to ferry supplies under the cover of darkness.

Supported by well-trained pilots and aircrews, and a stateside manufacturing base that had an inexhaustible capacity to produce airplanes, the heroes of air war Europe—the B-17, B-24, B-25, A-20, PV-1, P-47, P-51, P-39, P-40, and P-38— plus a new plane, the B-29, continued the war in the Pacific. Augmenting this daunting arsenal were staggering numbers of Navy and Marine Corps fighters, dive bombers, and torpedo bombers—including the SBD Dauntless dive bomber, SB2-C Helldiver, TBF/TBM Avenger torpedo bomber, and the F4F Wildcat, F4U Corsair, and F6F Hellcat fighters. Add to these the highly effective patrol bombers such as the Convair PB4Y-2 Privateer, PV-2 Harpoon, PBY Catalina, and other oddities, such as a squadron of Marine Corps Leathernecks flying B-25s, and

Marine TBF gunners talk among themselves as they wait for their pilots to come out of a briefing before a strike against Rabaul. Land-based marines destroyed 2,439 Japanese aircraft in air-to-air combat.

you have a force the size and diversity of which would go unmatched until the Persian Gulf War of 1991.

Because of the tight spaces of the Pacific, and the reliance on ships and shipping, the war could be particularly cruel. Fires were a constant.

A rising plume of black smoke marked the horror of raging fires on ships as they succumbed to bombs and torpedoes, oftentimes at the cost of hundreds of men perishing in their hulls. Similarly, streaks of brilliant white traced the final moments of a plane as it fell across the sky, while other plumes of smoke would mark the crash of a crippled bomber or fighter.

For the enemy, fire itself was often the weapon that sent them to their deaths. The torch of a flame thrower, the flaming gell of napalm in the incendiary bombs of the strategic bombing campaigns, and, of course, the vaporizing heat of the atomic bombs. The low-level incendiary attacks pioneered by General Curtis E. LeMay and his B-29s triggered firestorms in every major Japanese target of military importance. Tokyo. Kobe. Nagoya. Osaka. Yokohama. Kawasaki. Fukuoka. Tsuruga. Musashi. Over 25,500 individual bomber sorties were flown from the Marianas against Japan, often targeting a city until it was gone. Bomb damage assessments had a new column: how many square miles had been reduced to embers? Kobe, to give but one example, was so thoroughly burned-out that it was ultimately taken off the targeting list as "not worth revisiting."

Water is to fire as Yin is to Yang, but, in the Pacific, water was not always a friend. On land, the suffocating humidity and the sweltering 100-degree heat combined with the drenching rains to create conditions that were as deadly as combat. Dysentery, malaria, and dengue fever; the insects and snakes that bred in fetid pools of water; and the open sores called jungle rot—all these took their toll as surely as bullets. One post-battle assessment of Guadalcanal stated that at any given

Pilots in the ready room, USS Ticonderoga.

time during the six months of fighting, 10 to 15 percent of our forces were incapacitated by disease. For battles as close as those, 10 percent could have easily been the deciding factor.

Then there was the ocean itself. Romantic, blue, and suffused with childhood images of an idyllic life, the ocean was anything but. Like the pearls of a necklace, the islands of the Pacific stretched 3000 miles across vast open seas but the islands were small, hard to find, prone to bad weather, and most did not have runways. In Germany, a battle-damaged bomber had but a few hundred miles to overcome, all of it over land, in order to limp home. In the Pacific, it was often a 7-hour flight over open seas—extreme circumstances under some conditions, an impossibility under others. If a bomber couldn't make it back, and the excellent sea-air rescue services couldn't find the crew, the sea would silently claim another dozen men.

Then, as in all wars, there was luck, good and bad. One bomber would come home unscathed; another would suffer a direct hit by flak and be instantly blown apart. Many pictures in this book tell this story, but one in particular illustrates the role of luck. On a dark, foggy night men were fast asleep on the island of Tinian. Somewhere out to sea, inside a battered B-29, was another group of

men hanging on for dear life. The cabin creaked and strained against the jolts of a Pacific thunderstorm, and the sea seemed certain to be their last landing when somehow they reached Tinian. Desperate, the pilot made a blind plunge for the airfield. The bomber plowed across the sands, nearly sheered off a wing, and careened to a stop on a ridge, its fuselage ripped open. It was again

Young, anxious faces before a mission. In the ready room aboard the new USS Yorktown *(the previous* Yorktown *was sunk at the battle of Midway).*

A P-51 pilot and his crew chief prepare for a mission. Iwo Jima.

quiet on the island. But one man on the ground was killed and two others injured when their tents were plowed down by this bomber. That is war.

This book is a telling of the air war in pictures. It was the intention of this author to organize in one place the most compelling images of the air war so we may look back and see the conflict the way it was experienced—raw and unadorned, a terrible conflict that cost many lives and was won by men who did it not for glory but because it was asked of them. This book leaves to others the written history of the campaigns; rather, it tells a story words alone cannot convey.

In terms of sheer numbers, the photographs of World War II retained by the National Archives are utterly staggering. According to the official records published by the Archives there are 785,675 war photographs from the Navy, 406,266 from the Marine Corps, and approximately 500,000 from the Air Force. That doesn't include the more prodigious output of the Army Signal Corps (more than one-million photographs) nor the tens of thousands of pictures from the Coast Guard.

After narrowing one's search to a topic such as this book, one is still immersed in a cinerama of photos, and therein lies an education separate from a study of the war's textual records. Picture after picture of ground battles, airfields under attack, mechanics and pilots, and hundreds of photographs of aircraft carriers under attack (some burning, some enveloped in flames, some lost to kamikazes, some just lost) tell us about the war in quite a different way. Although the media is absolutely still and utterly silent we sense the emotions of war—love, hate, loneliness, horror, fear, helplessness, death—and we begin to see the totality of the conflict. We can read that the *Yorktown* was sunk at Midway; we can *see* it happen in the photographs. It is quite different.

Island after island, battle after battle, the photographs show us the war—formation after formation of bombers departing, enroute, bombing, and landing; the flak-riddled aircraft, the crash landings, the heroics; the carrier battles, the medium bombers in ground attack; the bombs and torpedoes finding their mark; the ships sinking; and, in the end, the celebratory flights. The pieces come together. Today, far

An underwing shot of one of the B-25s, designated as PBJs, flown by the Marine Corps. This plane is attached to the 4th Marine Aircraft Wing then based on Iwo Jima. It is armed with rockets and rigged for night attacks on shipping.

too many glamorize the war; equally, many have become obsessed with the details. Is it a Zero or a Betty or a Jill, a light destroyer or a frigate? The pilots didn't care; neither did the photographer—no such detail spurred either to press the button. Rather, this was battle. The pilot was destroying the enemy and the photographer was capturing the moment, the savagery, the violence, the unfolding of a drama. We miss that in statistics; we find that in photography. We find even more when we examine the pictures closely.

There are some gaps in the photographic records from the Pacific. Unlike the war in Europe, combat photography from the air war in the Pacific was surprisingly limited in many categories. For instance, we have far fewer photographs taken during the actual bombing missions than we do in Europe, and it is also rare to find air-to-air photography from inside attacking American aircraft. Perhaps the length of the missions or the distances back to the media outlets in New York City explain this. (The use of radio waves to transmit photographs was refined by the Signal Corps and used to send images home from the Pacific; the first electronic images sent back to the United States were photographs of the raids on Rabaul.)

Japanese gun camera footage is also largely missing. While we have an abundance of images from German gun cameras, in over a year of researching this author failed to find even one from Japanese cameras. One can speculate why but in the end they were simply not there.

The war in the Pacific was hard, brutal, hot, humid, violent, terrifying—and fought on ground alien to the American soldier. Through the selection of photographs in this book it is the hope of the author that readers will in some small way understand what hundreds of thousands of men endured for the sake of this nation. Many of these photographs have never before been published while others are classics and familiar to students of World War II. But viewed as a collection they provide a unique portrait of a time one hopes is never repeated again.

GEOGRAPHY

The geography of the Pacific is not well understood even today. The map at the right is an official 1942 U.S. Army map of the region. It is useful not only to place distant islands but also to gain a perspective on how large, dispersed, obscure, and, militarily, indefensible the Japanese perimeter was in the Pacific Theater. By early 1942, the Japanese had occupied islands as far south as New Guinea (a scant few miles from Australia) and the Solomons, the western coast of China and French Indochina (now Vietnam, Cambodia, and Laos), the island chains of the South Pacific, and as far north as the Aleutians.

As we ramped up for war, time was precious—the Japanese were aiming to expand even further, expansion that if successful would have pushed our staging areas back as far as Hawaii. We immediately faced a crisis on the eastern tip of New Guinea at Port Moresby, where the Japanese threatened to close our supply route to Australia. This route traces a line to the east of the Solomon Islands via the Ellice Islands. It is easy to see on a map how the occupation of

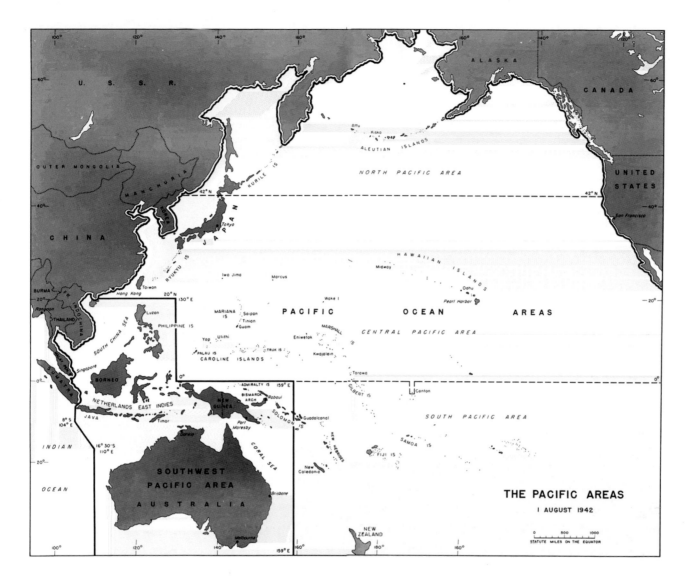

THE PACIFIC AREAS
1 AUGUST 1942

Port Moresby would have all but blocked that route–and a Japanese airfield on Guadalcanal worked to seal it closed. Thus, the first three engagements in the Pacific were driven by the geography. We fought to protect our toeholds— the Battle of the Coral Sea, which ultimately prevented the Japanese from occupying Port Moresby; the Battle of Midway, to preserve our positions flanking Hawaii; and then the invasion of Guadalcanal, to stop the occupation and the building of a Japanese airfield there. By preserving Midway and Port Moresby and by taking Guadalcanal, we were well positioned to begin the advances up from Australia and through the Central Pacific towards Japan. From there, the geographic landmarks would be a succession of small islands in the South Pacific until a "front" was established in the Marianas.

CHAPTER 2

AMERICA ENGAGES JAPAN

The war in the Pacific began and ended as an air war. Pearl Harbor.

Doolittle's raid on Tokyo. The atomic bombing of Japan.

The war in the Pacific, according to U.S. Navy historians could be divided into three phases. The first stage was the "Japanese offensive," which ran from December 7, 1941 through June 1942 (Midway). The second stage was the "offensive-defensive" stage. This ran from August 1942 (the invasion of Guadalcanal) to November 1943 (the taking of Torokina on Bougainville). Then came the true "Allied offensive," September 1943 (the initial strikes against Tarawa and Makin in the Gilberts) through the Japanese surrender in September 1945. Through each stage, air power gained strength. Often as not, the first thrusts were made by carrier-based aircraft. Two aircraft carriers were used to engage the Japanese at Coral Sea, successfully halting their advance to Port Moresby but losing the *Lexington*. At Midway, we used the carriers *Enterprise, Yorktown,* and *Hornet* to halt the Japanese on our flanks, at the cost of the *Yorktown*. The invasion of Guadalcanal was covered by three aircraft carriers, and during the campaign the *Enterprise* and *Saratoga* were damaged and we lost the *Hornet* and the *Wasp,* although by then we had our first land-based air forces permanently stationed on a formerly-occupied island.

Often overlooked in the many portraits of the air war was success in air-to-air combat of the patrol bombers. Originally compiled in the 1947 study *Naval Aviation Combat Statistics—World War II* by the Office of Naval Intelligence, and subsequently updated in 1976, patrol aircraft are credited with 386 air-to-air kills. VPB-117 led the list with 58 kills. Eight separate aircraft crews were credited with five or more shoot-downs; had these crews been officially recognized, they would have qualified as air aces. Five of the eight "aces" were from VPB-117. The patrol aircraft included in this study were the PBY Catalina, PV Ventura, PBM Mariner, PB2Y Coronados, and, with 323 of the kills, the PB4Y-1 Liberator and PB4Y-2 Privateer. Japanese aircraft kills credited to patrol bombers ranged from Zeros, Vals, and Bettys to seaplanes such as the Mavis, Emily, and the single engine Jake.

*P-47 Thunderbolts take to the air. Red lights and
stop signs at each end of the strip warn ground crews
of departures.*

A tight formation of B-29s over Iwo Jima.

Screaming through a fusillade of antiaircraft fire, a Japanese Jill bomber bears down on the fleet near Truk. However close she appears to completing a successful pass, the plane was destroyed before releasing her torpedo. This exceptionally clear, two-shot series captures the intensity of war at sea and the ferocious hail of fire that came up to meet Japanese and Navy flyers alike.

Two B5N Kates from the Zuikaku Air Group make a low-level pass on the USS South Dakota at the Battle of the Santa Cruz Islands on October 26, 1942.

A Kate sweeps in to release a torpedo against the Hornet.

The torpedo splashes into the water as the plane makes a low pass over the bridge of the Hornet.

The USS Enterprise *under attack.*

Used in countless books, this well-known but dramatic photograph shows an attacking Zero sawed in half by antiaircraft fire as it tries in vain to score a hit on an American ship.

Fires burn out of control on the USS Wasp *following a torpedo attack by a Japanese submarine. The* Wasp *sank on September 15, 1943.*

Kates and Vals work over the USS Hornet. On this page, two Kates make low passes as a Val plummets in a suicide dive into the Hornet's deck.

The Val crashes into the signal bridge of the Hornet. When the war was over, Admiral Nimitz would say that of all the Japanese tactics and weapons, he feared the kamikazes most. Technically, the Val aiming for the deck of the Hornet was not officially a kamikaze but rather a precursor—and an ominous one at that. The Kamikaze Corps were not formally organized until the fall of 1944, but as this pilot clearly demonstrates, it was woven into the Japanese psyche, if not their oaths as soldiers, to die for their country.

Right: This well-known but often miscaptioned picture was taken on the deck of the USS Yorktown. The Yorktown, which was rushed from Pearl Harbor to join the fight at Midway after a hasty 48-hour repair job, has suffered three direct bomb hits and two torpedoes. She is, as this photograph was taken, listing precariously and all but doomed. According to the notes accompanying the original photograph, the men are lining the deck not to make repairs, which is how this picture is often captioned, but to evacuate. The Yorktown was abandoned and later sunk by a Japanese sub. Midway was a turning point for America. The Japanese lost four carriers and 330 planes during the battle. America had bloodied the invincible forces of Japan.

From his battle station, a sailor on the USS South Dakota watches the USS Bunker Hill as it burns in the distance.

Note that two aircraft, probably Vals, are going down in this picture, one seen just moments before hitting the sea and the other, in the background, trailing fire.

Below and facing page, right, top: *The telltale signatures of combat at sea. A streak of fire in the sky, a plume of smoke rising from the ocean—each marks the death of a Japanese aircraft.*

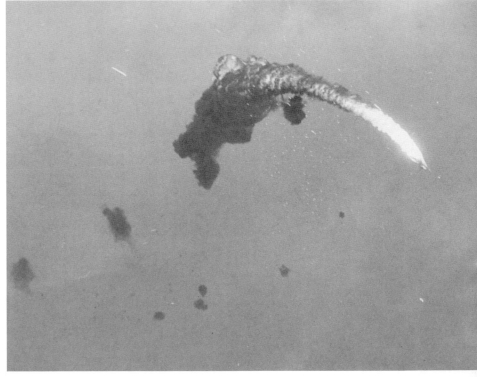

Signs held high on the flight deck give final instructions to Navy TBF pilots as they take off from the USS Enterprise *during the Santa Cruz battle. In the middle, one sign reads "JAP CV, Speed 25 knots" while the other, to the right, speaks of the devastating damage to the carrier USS* Hornet. *It reads "Proceed without* Hornet." *Shortly after this photograph was taken, the* Enterprise *too was hit but she soldiered on, recovering aircraft from both carriers.*

The largest and reputedly one of the most heavily-armed seaplanes built by either side, a Japanese Emily, is brought down.

A Japanese Jill torpedo bomber. The original photograph was without captions and thus it is unclear whether the plane was hit by antiaircraft fire or during an air-to-air engagement. The date on this picture however suggests that it was taken during the campaign for the Marianas but before the famous Marianas Turkey Shoot when, in one day, Allied fighters downed more than 300 Japanese aircraft at a cost of roughly 30 of our own. As the flames from the wing root suggest, her fuel tanks are ablaze. On the right, the Jill is inverted and going away from the camera.

Four Bettys from the 5th Attack Force in Rabaul skim the surface of the ocean to evade antiaircraft fire as they attack American ships near Guadalcanal. The fourth aircraft is barely visible in the background. August 8, 1942.

Before the engine is started, mechanics turn the prop a few times to clear the gas lines. Henderson Field, Guadalcanal, June 1943.

Marine Corps F4U Corsairs prepare to take off in support of the fighting on the beachhead at Bougainville on November 1, 1943. These fighters are based on the island of Vella Lavella in the northern Solomons. The field was cut out of the jungle by Navy Seabees.

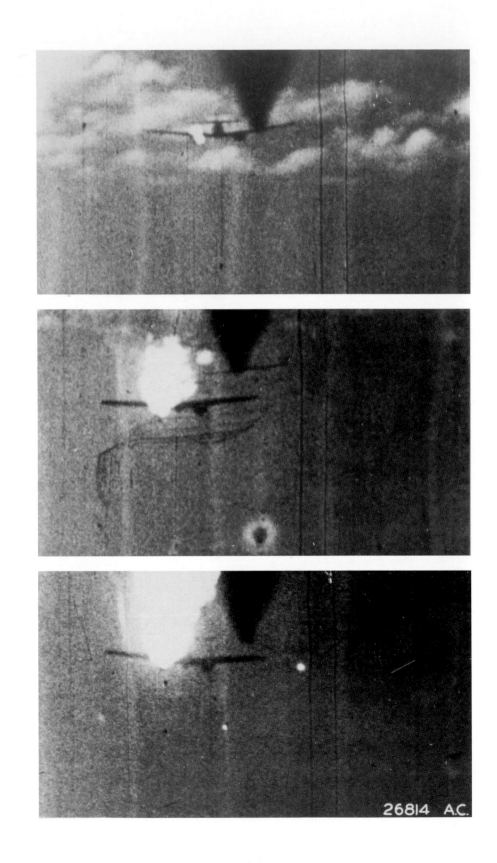

Left: *The left fuel tank on a Japanese Dinah is ignited by the guns of a P-38. The alignment pip of the plane's camera appears at the top of this photograph to be a second plane, which it is not. Wewak, New Guinea.*

Above: *A Japanese Mavis is caught from above by a Navy patrol bomber in Tokyo Bay.*

As one pilot would dryly state in an after action report for a mission during which 10 Japanese floatplanes were shot down, "With six .50-caliber guns going into a propeller and an engine it's going to be disastrous no matter whose engine and whose propeller it is." In this series of photographs an F6F Hellcat dives on a Jake near Saipan and, with that firepower, scores a kill.

The Betty carried a seven-man crew and was well armed both nose and tail, which our pilots adapted to by attacking from above. In fact, some squadrons issued their pilots specific orders not to attack Bettys except in "steep high-side passes or a good overhead pass" to avoid "the stinger in the tail." Because the Betty had little armor and no self-sealing tanks, the aiming point was between the fuselage and the engine mount, not the cockpit. Said one pilot, whose comment is well illustrated on these pages, "We always shot at one of those gas tanks in the wing. Most of the time the wing itself would look like it had caught fire. Eventually the wing will lose enough strength until it breaks off or the Japanese pilot—he has to go down."

This series of photographs captures just how effective this tactic was. This Betty is brought down by a PV Ventura off the island of Truk. The Ventura spotted the enemy, jettisoned her depth charges, and descended on the bomber, wheeling around as her guns aimed for the wing root.

Looking much like our own C-47, this Japanese Tabby (a licensed version of the American DC-3, a few of which were codenamed Tess) was caught by a Navy patrol bomber and quickly shot down.

A Navy Liberator intercepts a Betty near Truk. Liberators, and then Privateers, were commonly used by the Navy to defend the perimeter when surface ships were engaged in a landing.

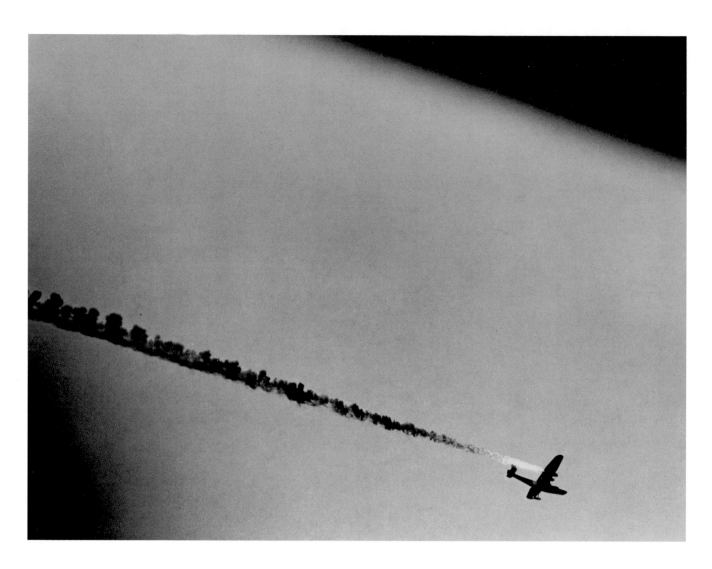

Her engine streaming fire and smoke, a Mavis goes down.

Gun camera footage of an air-to-air engagement against a Japanese Zero. Seen from a Hellcat.

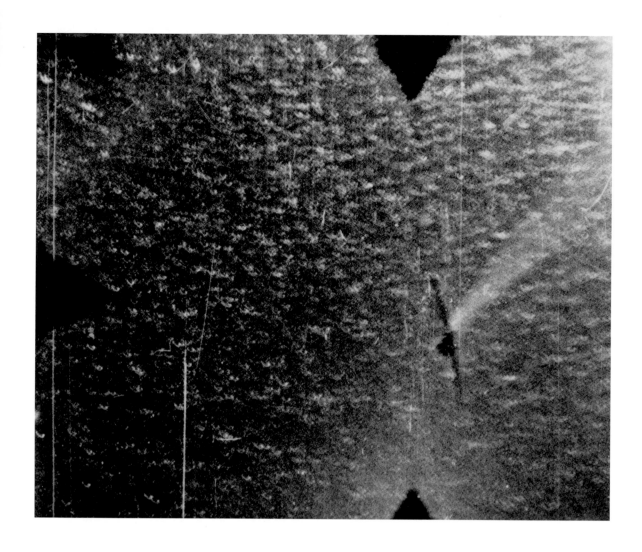

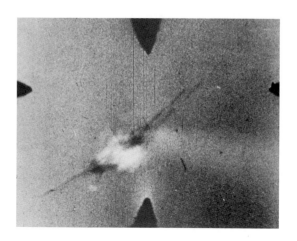

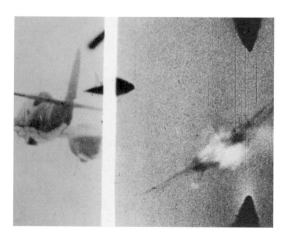

Left: A Japanese Lily is intercepted by a P-39 over New Guinea.

Right: *These two photos capture the final moment before another Betty hits the sea.*

Left: *Exceptionally clear footage of two different Bettys under attack. In both engagements, the Navy patrol bombers attacked from above, circling their targets and aiming for the fuselage. Bullets slam into the Betty's fuselage as the medium bomber attempts to escape. Finding her fuel tanks, fire breaks out along her left wing root.*

Dramatic footage of a Japanese Mavis being brought down by a patrol bomber.

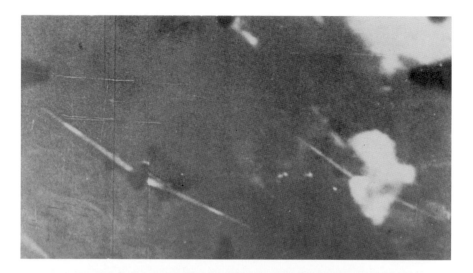

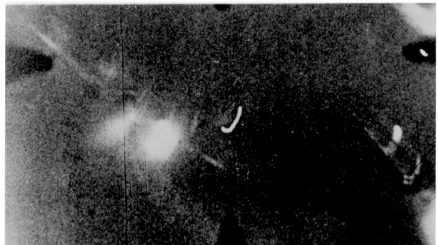

Gun cameras on a P-39 record the kill of two Japanese Lily aircraft in a row.

*A Japanese Sally bursts into flames after being hit
by bullets from the guns on a Navy Liberator.*

The American fighter pilot entered the Pacific with good training but absolutely no combat experience. They faced a dedicated, combat-hardened Japanese aviator with as much as twice the time in the air. The absence of armor and self-sealing tanks made the wonderfully maneuverable Japanese planes vulnerable, which was of significant help in the early years, but as the war wore on the sheer numbers of American aviators, the constant training and retraining, and the improvements in aircraft such as the P-38, F4U Corsair, and the venerable F6F Hellcat, helped turn the tide. One lesser known example of training in the forward areas was the use of utility squadrons to improve gunnery skills. Throughout the first years of the war, utility squadrons moved into the forward areas to help pilot's fine tune their air-to-air gunnery accuracy. Using the latest radio-controlled drones and towed targets, improved techniques were taught to the Army, Navy, and Marine Corps fighter pilots in the lulls between battles.

CHAPTER 3

ISLAND HOPPING

As Allied forces island hopped towards Japan, air power was used in the close air support role, against convoys, to fly cover over the amphibious forces, and to attack air bases such as those at Rabaul. For our light and medium bombers, such as the A-20 and B-25, these were some of the most dangerous missions of the war. To interdict troop transports, enemy tankers, resupply convoys, and other Japanese shipping, our bombers came in low and often faced gauntlets of withering fire from the ships they were attacking and from antiaircraft guns placed on the hills encircling the harbors and inlets.

The montage of photos beginning on the following page and through page 63 were, according to a handwritten notation, a series of photos used in the "Third Report of the C.G. of the AAF to the Secretary of War." These pictures were selected to show the generals back in Washington, D.C. conclusive, dramatic, and extraordinarily blunt proof of the violence of air power against Japanese shipping. Taken together, they illustrate the incredible effectiveness of low level attack and the brutal accuracy of skip bombing. Viewed today, sixty years later, they show even more. This series of bomber-versus-destroyer photographs epitomizes the dogged, winner-take-all character of combat. Here we see soldiers pitting their wits and skills against each other in engagements where one ship or one airplane most surely would die. It is man-versus-man, machine-versus-machine. It is war.

Over the next six pages B-25s go head-to-head with a prime target—Japanese destroyers, most of them the smaller escort destroyers. Many of these pictures were taken in Ormoc Bay at Leyte in the Philippines. B-25s have intercepted a convoy and attack it mercilessly. They drop bombs and strafe the decks as they strike again and again and again.

A few different ships are captured in the lenses of the photographers; many of the B-25s were of the 345th Bomb Group, better known as the Air Apaches.

Parachute-retarded fragmentation bombs were used with great effectiveness in the Pacific. Fragmentation bombs could ignite precious fuel supplies or destroy ground aircraft without scoring a direct hit. The chutes delayed the explosions long enough for the low-flying bomber to clear the blast area.

Japanese ships are strafed and bombed as Allied forces move forward. Inlets, coves, and harbors such as these were surrounded by land-based antiaircraft guns.

THE NAVAL WAR IN THE PACIFIC DURING 1944

(Distances are in nautical miles)

The year 1944 saw a great amphibious offensive unfold in the Pacific. The forces . . . spearheaded and sustained by the United States Pacific Fleet drove in massive lunges through Japan's ill-gotten conquests, moving 1830 miles westward from Tarawa and Makin to anchor their armed night securely in the Marianas. From there systematic bombarding of Tokyo and other Japanese industrial centers has begun.

From the jungles of New Britain the front was pushed 1600 miles north and west to the Philippines. To U. S. offensive forces in the Marianas and Philippines, as elsewhere in the Pacific, a constant procession of cargo vessels is carrying thousands of tons of supplies. These two points are 4938 miles and 6056 miles, respectively, from San Francisco. No military operation has ever embraced such dimensions.

During 1944, 6,650 enemy aircraft were destroyed in the Pacific Ocean Areas. Of these approximately 5,450 were destroyed by carrier aircraft, and 1,200 by land-based airplanes. Of the year's total, approximately 3,975 enemy aircraft were destroyed in the air, and 2,675 on the ground. These figures also do not include reports from the Southwest Pacific command.

No review of the year would be complete without mention of our land-based air forces. As we have moved the battlefront steadily across the Pacific, we have drawn after us a net of air and surface blockade, entangling, pinning down, choking the by-passed Japanese holdings. An estimated 225,000 enemy troops, and strong enemy bastions such as Truk, Kavieng and Rabaul, have been reduced to impotence or to ashes.

In addition to ceaseless patrolling by surface units, many hundreds of land-based air strikes have been necessary to enforce this blockade. Many of these strikes were in force, with heavy bomb loads dropped on important targets. Others were small. When practicable they were closely coordinated with carrier-based attacks and amphibious landings. Together with our surface patrolling, these air strikes destroyed enemy strength in by-passed zones and made possible our rapid advance.

The year 1944 has brought success and added momentum to our advancing forces. But the Pacific is an ocean of fantastic distances. The road to Tokyo is rough and long. The enemy has just begun to defend his Home Empire. We have just begun to meet the tremendous problems of logistics, of supplying our forces—problems that grow greater with every forward step.

The decisive battles, the greatest battles, the hardest battles of the war in the Pacific are still to come. They must be fought with supreme effort on the part of all of us; in factories throughout our country, across the long sea lanes, and in the forward areas where the men of all our armed services, and those of our Allies, are fighting—for the enemy, like ourselves, has just begun to fight.

The captain of this destroyer has zigzagged through the waters to avoid the B-25s but considerable damage has already been done. The destroyer burns, three or more men lay on the main deck, and shells from the ship's aft 4-inch gun litter the deck. The B-25 has its bomb bay doors open and what appears to be a bomb is falling towards the ship.

The attack continues with two bombers visible in this photograph. The second one is obscured but can be seen to the left just below the horizon. The blurred objects in the upper left hand corner are probably .50-caliber shell casings.

*Another low-level bombing of a Japanese destroyer.
Three sailors, one dead, are behind the aft 4-inch
gun. Two more men are visible amidships.*

The B-25s score a decisive direct hit.

A near miss on an already foundering destroyer.

B-58114 A.C

62

Bombs bracket a light destroyer.

Two bombs tumble through the air towards a Japanese-held railroad bridge over what is identified as the Song Thong River in Indochina.

A Japanese Helen caught on the ground and destroyed during the battle of Wewak, New Guinea. A rack of bombs sits to the right of the bomber indicating that it was being readied for takeoff. The photograph was taken during a low-level bombing mission by B-25s.

A bombed-out hanger can be seen in the wake of a
B-25 over Wotje Island, the Marshall Islands.

Three B-25s make a high-speed pass down a bombed-out Japanese airstrip in Wewak. Notice the camouflaged Japanese airplanes along the far side of the runway.

A-20s make a low level parafrag pass over rail lines on Luzon, Philippines. Note that the bomb bay doors are open.

Parafrags descend on Clark Field in the Philippines during the fighting that led to General MacArthur's return.

Bombs descend on camouflaged rail cars on Luzon. Static lines are visible streaming behind the airplane.

A Japanese tanker carrying refined gasoline is cornered in a small Indochina inlet and successfully attacked by B-25s. Note the spreading fuel.

A flight of attackers heads towards the Japanese on Munda Field in the Solomons. The Grumman TBF is carrying a 2,000-pound bomb.

An SB2-C has just released a 1,000-pound bomb during an attack on a Japanese convoy.

ACTION REPORT

A DAY IN THE AIR WAR

TENTH AF

28 FBs spt ground forces around Hosi and Molo. 12 B-25s knock out Mong Pawn bridge. 8 P-47s damage approach to Pa-mao bridge. 8 others hit Hsumhsai A/F. 90-plus FBs hit troops, supplies, vehicles, ferry crossing, and various T/Os at several locations including Nauchye, Hsenwi, Man Pwe, Pongkalau, Nawng Mawn, Na-lang, Kunhkan, and Panghtu-lin. 550 transport sorties are flown to forward areas.

2/1/45
FOURTEENTH AF

6 B-24s attack shipping off Indochina coast, claiming 1 cargo vessel sunk and a patrol boat damaged. 4 P-40s attack div HQ SW of Yungning.

2/1/45
FEAF

B-24s pound Canacao peninsula and Cavite areas. Tgts include shipyard, seaplane base, comm, and supply. B-25s hit Puerto Princesa. B-24s bomb Okayama A/F during 31 Jan/1 Feb and hit Okayama and Heito A/F and Toko seaplane base during the following day.

2/1/45
TWENTIETH AF

67 B-29s bomb the Admiralty IX Floating Drydock (and vessel berthed in it) at Singapore navy yard. 21 other B-29s bomb West Wall area of the naval base. 21 others hit alternate tgts at Martaban and George Town.

—from The Army Air Forces in World War II

An overwing shot shows ships maneuvering while under attack during the Battle of the Solomon Islands, November 16, 1942.

Marine dive bombers hit enemy fuel stores near Rabaul. Rabaul was a major Japanese air base strategically located off the coast of New Guinea within easy striking distance of Allied forces on Guadalcanal, Port Moresby, and Bougainville, as well as surface ships in the slot between the Admiralty Islands and the Caroline Islands. Rabaul was reinforced with facilities for as many as 1,000 aircraft, and from Rabaul attacks were mounted against the American forces during the campaign for Guadalcanal, where the pilot in this photograph was based.

Two P-38s form up on a B-25.

A light destroyer bracketed by bombs. Near Hokkaido, Japan.

CHAPTER 4

STRATEGIC BOMBING

An invasion of mainland Japan was thought to be a necessary precursor to the end of the war. Just as one would prepare for any invasion, the landing would be preceded by bombing. Bombing of industrial targets. Bombing of military targets. And Bombing of shore targets. In November 1944, B-29s based in the Marianas began that bombing.

While the B-17 (until early 1943), and to a greater extent the B-24, were used extensively in the Pacific (the USAAF had 6,000 B-24s), the B-29 did the heavy lifting in the strategic endgame. The only bomber with the range to reach Japan from the bases in the Marianas (Guam, Saipan, and Tinian), the B-29 was the primary bomber used against the mainland. At first, however, the B-29 seemed to be the wrong plane for the mission. Unlike over Germany, high-altitude precision bombing didn't seem to be working over Japan. With B-29s bombing from 30,000 feet, less than 10 percent of payloads found their mark. Moreover, engines were failing. Many thought the B-29 itself was the problem, but there were unusual winds criss-crossing mainland Japan, including a 200- to 400-mile-per-hour wind that was not present over Europe—the jetstream.

On March 9, 1945, the bombing tactic was changed. B-29s would try bombing at night, from as low as 7,000 feet, using incendiary bombs. The tactic had every reason to succeed. The Japanese did not have a credible night-fighting air force and their antiaircraft fire was poor due to inadequate radar. The lower altitudes avoided the winds and reduced the strain on the engines, thus minimizing operational losses. Tokyo was the target on that first night and 1,676 tons of bombs were dropped on sites generally industrial in nature. The ensuing firestorm consumed almost 16 square miles of the city. Nagoya, Osaka, Kobe, and Kawasaki were targeted next with good result. Between March 9 and March 19, a total of 1,595 sorties delivered 9,373 tons of bombs at a cost of just 22 airplanes. Through the end of the war, more than 66 Japanese cities were bombed.

A gunner on a B-24 during a raid over Wake Island.

58284

High among cumulus-like clouds of smoke, B-29s bomb the city of Kobe, Japan. The city was targeted for its numerous factories supporting the Japanese war effort.

Left: These B-29s flew over Kobe at low altitude during the night, and, ultimately, during the day, too. To husband their increasingly limited aviation resources for the expected land invasion, the Japanese often kept their fighters on the ground.

A Japanese Nick makes a frontal attack on a formation of B-29s over Japan, passing perilously close beneath the bomber at the top of the picture.

According to military records, this is one of the first photographs of an air-dropped phosphorous bomb. Phosphorous bombs were used extensively by the Japanese. They were either fired up from ground batteries or dropped from above on the bomber formations. The air-dropped bombs had a five-second fuse. Air-to-air bombing dates back to World War I.

A phosphorous bomb explodes in the middle of a formation of B-24s over Truk, the Carolinas. Truk was the major Japanese naval base in the Central Pacific.

A B-29 continues its bombing run with one engine feathered.

A Japanese Zero crashes into a B-24 Liberator. The B-24 was part of a bomber group intercepted over Los Negros Island. While this looks like a suicide attack, flyers in the formation would later say that the Zero made a tail pass and was unable to pull out. The photograph was taken at the instant of the collision. The nose of the Zero can be seen to the right of the Liberator's collapsing wing. Both planes then exploded and crashed.

A B-29 is hit by flak and hurtles toward the ground. One wing is gone.

A Japanese Oscar jumps a B-25 attacking a small convoy in Hansa Bay, New Guinea.

Antiaircraft fire scores a direct hit on a B-29. Pieces fly off the mortally-wounded bomber as it tumbles towards the ground.

A Japanese phosphorous bomb bursts over a formation of B-24s over Iwo Jima. The B-24s were softening the island in advance of the invasion.

A Zero attacks a formation of B-24s.

This photograph tells more than one story. A B-29 waist gunner has been sucked out of his shot-away gun blister and now dangles by one leg five miles above Tokyo. According to the press release the gunner lost consciousness and suffered frostbite but was pulled to safety by his crewmembers. The other story? It is unlikely that this photography accurately depicts the drama. It is clear that this photograph was retouched. White lines create a balled-up form of an airman but in an anatomically impossible position. The retouching probably made the picture more acceptable for the home front.

A flight of B-24s release bombs over Truk.

The original USAAF caption, written in 1945, merits repeating verbatim. It says: "In a setting of cathedral-like majesty, this B-29 Superfortress of the 314th Air Wing is about to go down near Kobe, Japan." No doubt the public affairs officer saw beauty in the juxtapositioning of elements but the loss of an aircrew over enemy territory is a tragedy.

There can be no doubt that war is intensely personal, as this moment in battle illustrates with sickening finality. A flight of two A-20 Havocs descend on an inlet in New Guinea. One emerges unscathed . . .

. . . but the other is hit by antiaircraft fire and slams into the sea.

The surviving Havoc can do nothing for the lost crew. The shot-down bomber has disintegrated upon impact. The sting of such moments is remembered even today when pilots recount the unbearable pain they felt as they helplessly watched friends die.

B-29s release incendiary bombs over Yokohama, Japan. May 25, 1945.

Raid on the Nakajima Aircraft plant in Ota, Japan. Nakajima built many of Japan's well-known fighters.

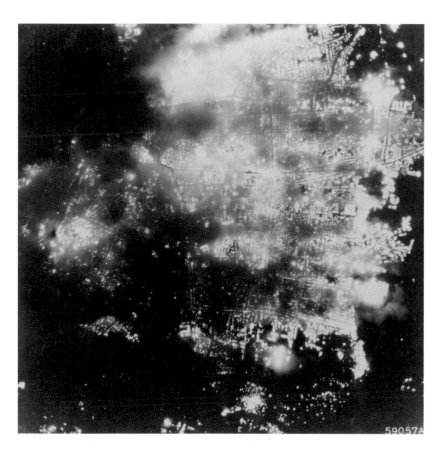

Incendiary bombing of Toyama, Japan on the night of August 1, 1945.

Kobe, Japan. June 1945.

CHAPTER 5

GETTING HOME

There are many ways to measure the air war in the Pacific. American fighter pilots engaged tens of thousands of Japanese aircraft and shot down nearly 15,000 of them. Allied aircraft sunk 2,000,000 tons of shipping. Allied planes dropped 656,400 tons of bombs in the Pacific; B-29s accounted for 147,000 tons.

On an average day during the 88-day battle for Okinawa, 560 Allied planes were in the sky and fighting. All told, there were 896 Japanese air raids. During the campaign, aircraft launched 49,641 rockets, dropped 1,573 napalm bombs containing 260,000 gallons of gelled gasoline, and shot 9,000,000 rounds of ammunition. Land- and carrier-based aircraft flew 1,904 missions involving 17,361 individual sorties.

Staggering numbers, indeed.

After the battles, pilots had to land. Some aircraft were shot up and hard to control. Some were flown back to carriers that themselves were damaged. Some flight crews had to struggle across 1,500 miles of open ocean.

Air-sea rescue was integral to the war. In the early years, little could be done to rescue downed crews, something that changed during the Solomons and matured as the strategic bombing began from the Marianas. Navy Catalinas nicknamed Dumbos were used to pick up downed flyers in the Pacific. Many of these Dumbo pick-ups were made close to enemy shore positions.

In addition to the Catalinas, the Navy also used Mariners for open-sea rescues, as well as surface ships and submarines. (One such submarine, the *Tang,* is credited with recovering no less than 22 flyers off Truk.) During amphibious operations and landings, specific ships were positioned near the combat to rescue downed flyers.

For the bombing of the mainland, a chain of ships and subs was positioned on the route from the Marianas to Japan. When a plane went down, an assigned rescue aircraft, often a specially equipped B-29 or a Privateer, searched for survivors, dropped rafts, and then acted as the on-scene aerial rescue director. To give but one example of this system's effectiveness, in 1945 more than 2,000 airmen were rescued by the air-sea rescue services.

Still, getting home was dangerous. Many a tense ground crew searched the skies with anxious vigilance for the familiar sight of a bomber returning to an airfield or a Navy aircraft landing on a carrier.

Bombing Kuala Lumpur.

Ground crews wait on Iwo Jima.

Inside a B-24. Four crewmen drink canned grape-fruit juice and have a cigarette during the flight home. These four young men represent the sons and brothers and husbands that were the flesh and blood of the war.

SB2-Cs return to the USS Hancock *after strikes against Japanese convoys.*

A large formation of B-24 Liberators en route to their target, Cebu Island, in the Philippines.

This is the welcomed sight greeting a crew arriving home after a 3,000-mile round-trip mission to Japan. B-29s inbound to North Field, Guam. North Field and Northwest Field were the main airfields on Guam.

The 6,700-foot runway on Kwajalein in the Marshall Islands. Notice how basic the living quarters are. Tents dot the island from the lagoon to sea. More than 40 planes can be seen in this picture.

Final approach, Saipan.

Dense fog shrouded the island of Iwo Jima forcing this B-29 to ditch in the ocean. The B-29 was shot up over Tokyo and had come back with badly-wounded men on board.

Proving the bomber's durability—and no doubt the crew's good fortune—this B-29 survived a 1,500-mile, storm-tossed flight back from Tokyo with two engines out on one side. On landing, the bomber fell apart. The fuselage was severed by a runaway prop and during the crash the nose was completely sheared off. A relieved crew poses in front of the mangled wreckage on Saipan.

Weary airmen walk around the tail assembly of a B-29 after a surprise attack by the Japanese on Saipan.

This B-29 crashed at night while attempting a landing on Iwo Jima. On the ground one Seabee was killed and two men, asleep in their tents, were seriously injured.

Returning from a strike over Tokyo, a B-29 diverts to Iwo Jima for an emergency landing. The Superfortress careened into a line of P-51s after its brakes locked up. Four Mustangs were destroyed and five were damaged. Four members of the B-29's crew were injured, two seriously. In the foreground, men seek shelter from the heat, and the exploding ammunition, behind a jeep.

Nine B-29s diverted to Iwo Jima following a raid over Tokyo. This one had its controls shot away by flak and came to rest on the sand. Foxholes dot the foreground.

A mission was never over until the pilot walked away. A P-51 Mustang landing on Iwo Jima has flipped over and crashed into another P-51.

Men help an injured pilot make his way through the rubble at the end of the runway on Iwo Jima. The P-51 suffered an engine failure on take off and now smolders on the ground.

The brakes locked up as this B-25 landed at Port Moresby, New Guinea.

A pilot of a Fifth Air Force P-38 was badly injured when his brakes failed and the plane spun off the runway.

After this plane crashed in the jungles of New Guinea, the chief of a local village volunteered his men to help the Americans pull it out of the bush.

The Army photographer who shot this wreckage off the coast of New Guinea confidently identifies the aircraft as a B-25 Mitchell but few distinguishing features remain. The photograph is a stark reminder of how forbidding the islands of the Pacific could be.

No doubt shaken if not injured, the crew of this B-25 prepares a life raft as their bomber sinks. The crew was rescued by a Dumbo. Seen near the southern coast of the Philippines.

Racked with pain and terribly injured, the pilot of a shot-down A-20 is rescued by a Catalina even as Navy shells arced overhead during the pre-invasion bombardment of Corrigedor. The plane slammed down into Manila Bay breaking the nose, jaw, and cheekbones of this stoic aviator.

The war asked much of the air crews including the longest overwater flights recorded since the advent of military aviation. Here a PBY with the 13th Air Forces Emergency Rescue Group lands on the ocean near four survivors from a crashed B-24. The rescue took place near Peleliu. Notice the small sail on the raft.

This P-51 pilot went down while escorting B-29s en route to Japan. He has been picked up by a submarine positioned in the chain of ships and subs that stretched from Iwo Jima to the Japanese mainland.

A familiar if not nerve-wracking sight—a damaged B-29 attempting a landing. The Number 4 engine is out.

Wreckage of a B-29, a sheared-off engine in the foreground. Saipan.

Strikes by the Japanese against our air bases, such as seen here on Saipan, were executed with devastating effectiveness. Sixteen Zeros have destroyed three B-29s, while many more were damaged. Four charred motors and the tail assembly are all that remain of this Superfortress.

Returning from a mission over Japan and closing in on their air base, the crew of this B-29 faced sudden disaster when an engine caught fire. The pilot was unable to extinguish the flames but was within reach of the airstrip on the Marianas where he made a safe emergency landing.

Shocked, stunned, and barely able to walk, the pilot of this P-38 came down in flames and crash landed in the Philippines after being shot by a Zero over Mindora Island. A photographer snapped this incredible picture moments after the pilot pulled himself free.

On an otherwise calm day in the Marianas, ground crews noticed a B-29 heading towards the airfield. Low, slow, and obviously in trouble, their hearts sank as they watched the pilot struggle with the plane. The bomber drunkenly descended ever closer to the sea when it abruptly lost two engines and crashed. Every man that knew how to swim raced to the bomber to haul the crew out, many of whom were terribly injured. Despite these heroic efforts, three men were trapped in the plane and died.

Heroics were a constant theme of the war. Here men suffer the intense heat and risk of injury or death from exploding ammunition to push a flaming B-29 away from other aircraft.

The B-29 was an enormous airplane, something one sees with particular clarity in crash photography. The photographs on these pages show a B-29 after an emergency landing.

Right: The pilot of this P-38 Lightning was strafing Iwo Jima during the assault on the island when antiaircraft fire struck his tail boom and nearly severed his tail assembly. Had it done so, the plane would have spun into the ground. Instead, the P-38 held together and the pilot was able to climb out of the 50-foot attack and nurse his plane 700 miles home to the Marianas.

On landing, a Navy PB4Y-1 Liberator overruns the runway and ends up in the surf. Antiaircraft fire hit her hydraulics. The single-tail version of this aircraft was called the PB4Y-2 Privateer. The Navy received 977 Liberators and 739 Privateers.

A P-51 cracks up while landing on Iwo Jima.

*Men struggle to free the pilot of a P-51, which has
just crashed on Iwo Jima.*

The pilot of this P-38 is dazed after crashing on the island of Vella Lavella in the Solomon Islands. The P-38 was hit over Treasury Island and was forced to make a belly landing.

A seriously injured crew member is carried out of a B-24 following a raid on the Marshall Islands.

This badly shot-up F4F Wildcat missed the arresting wire as it attempted to land on a carrier. The runaway plane slammed into the aircraft parked on the flight deck, spun around, and continued to do damage until it struck the carrier's island and came to a halt. Injured men lay on the deck while others race to get out of the way.

Pilots would do anything to get back on board where crash trucks, rescue crews, and immediate medical attention were available.

The pilot in this F6F Hellcat curls up against the
intense heat as his aircraft burns on the carrier deck.
The skin of the plane is so hot that it blisters, yet fire
crews were able to pull him free. He suffered painful
burns but was able to walk away from the fire.

An F6F pilot barely makes it aboard the USS Bataan.

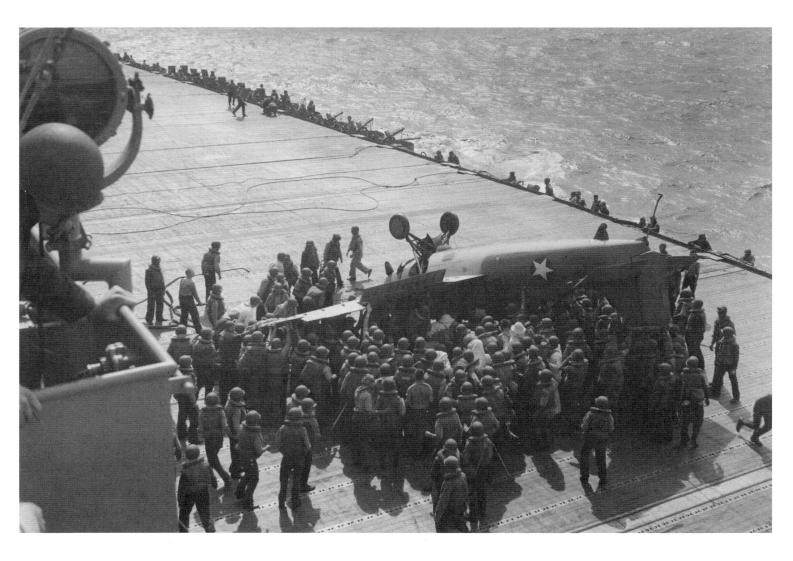

All hands rush to help extract the pilot of this F4F Wildcat after it flipped over during landing.

CHAPTER 6

VICTORY IN THE PACIFIC

As daylight broke over Hawaii on December 8, 1941, the United States seemed an unlikely victor in the war against Japan. Leading up to Pearl Harbor, our nation had just 593 aircraft operating in the Pacific, half of which were destroyed during the first weeks of December 1941.

Aviation assets at sea were no better. At the onset of hostilities, the Navy had just four aircraft carriers operating in the Pacific, a number reduced by half after Midway.

Worse still, American pilots went into battle with half the flight experience of the Japanese pilot and none of their combat experience.

Still, we fought—and in less than four years, Japan surrendered.

Victory in the Pacific was neither sweet nor joyous. The battles had been too vicious; the losses too painful. Japan was a tenacious foe and the bitterness that marked the conflict made victory little more than relief. The war was over. Men could go home. America could resume its life. That was enough.

Air power, though, played an incalculable role, as the following excerpt from the United States Strategic Bombing Survey (Pacific War) so succinctly notes:

Control of the air was essential to the success of every major military operation (in the Pacific). Control of the air enabled surface vessels to sail the seas as far as that control extended, even within range of enemy land-based airplanes. Control of the air permitted amphibious landings at any point where that control could be assured. Control of the air permitted close air support to ground forces, the effectiveness of which was decisive wherever fully employed. Control of the air over lines of communications permitted effective interdiction of them to the enemy and preserved them to ourselves. Control of the air over the Japanese home islands permitted the destruction by long-range bombing of such of her industries and cities as we chose to attack. The first objective of all commanders in the Pacific war, whether ground, sea or air, whether American, Allied, or Japanese, was to assure control of the air.

Control of the air was not easily achieved, and involved the coordinated application of all the resources of the nation. Air power consisted not merely of the planes and pilots that engaged the enemy, but of all the sources of strength that supported, reinforced and exploited control of the air. It was coordinated teamplay of ground, sea and air forces, both ground-based and carrier-based, and their supporting services, backed up by the full effort of all phases of the home front that enabled us to secure control of the air, at first locally and then more generally, culminating in virtual freedom of the skies over the Japanese home islands themselves.

Calm seas and a stunning sunset provide
a magnificent backdrop to a flight of P-51s
returning to Iwo Jima.

Henderson Field, Guadalcanal. SBDs in center foreground and TBFs to the right. B-17s are on the far side of the runway. In dead center is a PBY, and two more are at the far right.

Manila's South Harbor is littered with Japanese ships hit and sunk during the Allied retaking of the Philippines. In the foreground is a "stack aft" freighter of 4,400 gross tons. Approximately 20 ships are visible in this view of the harbor.

The burned-out shells of two Japanese bombers destroyed on the ground.

A lone B-17 taxis off the airstrip.
Henderson Field, Guadalcanal.

Central casting could hardly have done better. These handsome pilots of VF-17 let down their guard on Bougainville.

B-24s on the flight line on Eniwetok Island, in the Marshall Islands.

Old Glory snaps in the wind on Guadalcanal.

About the Author: Doug Keeney is the author of *Gun Camera World War II, The Doomsday Scenario,* and *Buddies: Men, Dogs and World War II*, as well as the author or co-author of six other military histories. Keeney has a B.A. in Economics from the University of Southern California and an M.B.A. from the University of Southern California Marshall School of Business. An avid tennis player and a licensed pilot, Keeney is a frequent researcher at the National Archives and in other military archives around the nation.

Left: *A formation of B-29s over Guam.*

THE JAPANESE OFFENSIVE

Dec 7, 1941	Japanese bomb Pearl Harbor, Wake Island, Guam, Philippines, and Midway
Dec 18, 1941	Japanese invade Hong Kong
Dec 22, 1941	Japanese invade Luzon, the Philippines
Dec 23, 1941	Japanese take Wake Island
Dec 25, 1941	Japanese take Hong Kong
Jan 19, 1942	Japanese take North Borneo
Jan 23, 1942	Japanese take Rabaul (New Britain, Solomon Islands)
Feb 15, 1942	Japanese take Singapore
Mar 18, 1942	Japanese take Java
Mar 11, 1942	Gen. MacArthur leaves Corregidor
Apr 9, 1942	U.S. surrenders at Bataan
May 3, 1942	Japanese take Tulagi (Guadalcanal Islands)
May 6, 1942	U.S. forces surrender; fall of Philippines

THE ALLIED OFFENSIVE

May 8, 1942	Battle of Coral Sea—U.S. carrier aircraft meet Japanese carrier aircraft in first battle at sea not involving ships. No clear victor.
June 5, 1942	U.S. forces defeat Japanese in Battle of Midway
Aug 7, 1942	U.S. forces invade Guadalcanal
Sept 27, 1942	British begin offensive in Burma
Jan 2, 1943	Allies advance in New Guinea
Feb 1, 1943	Japanese evacuate Guadalcanal
June 21, 1943	Allies advance to New Georgia, Solomon Islands
Aug 25, 1943	Allies take New Georgia
Nov 1, 1943	Allies land on Bougainville
Nov 20, 1943	Allies land on Tarawa
Dec 15, 1943	Allies land on New Britain
Jan 31, 1944	Allies take Kwajalein in the Marshall Islands
Feb 20, 1943	U.S. planes destroy Japanese bases at Rabaul and Truk
Feb 23, 1944	Allies begin attack on Marianas
June 15, 1944	U.S. lands on Saipan
June 19, 1944	Mariana "Turkey Shoot"
July 19, 1944	U.S. forces invade Guam
July 24, 1944	U.S. forces invade Tinian
Aug 8, 1944	Marianas under Allied control
Oct 11, 1944	Air raids start against Okinawa
Oct 26, 1944	Battle of Leyte Gulf
Oct 25, 1944	First kamikaze attacks
Nov 11, 1944	Iwo Jima
Feb 16, 1945	Recapture of Bataan
Feb 19, 1945	Invasion of Iwo Jima
Mar 2, 1945	Corregidor recaptured
Mar 3, 1945	Manila recaptured
April 1, 1945	Invasion of Okinawa
July 5, 1945	Liberation of Philippines
Aug 6, 1945	Hiroshima bombed
Aug 9, 1945	Nagasaki bombed
Sept 2, 1945	Japanese surrender on USS *Missouri*

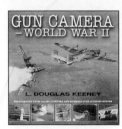

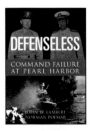